SPOTTER'S GUIDE

HORSES
& PONIES

Joanna Spector

Illustrated by David Wright,
Elaine Keenan and
Malcolm McGregor

Edited by Alastair Smith, Felicity Mansfield and Tim Dowley
Designed by Karen Tomlins and Joanne Kirkby
Series designer: Laura Fearn
Cover designer: Adam Constantine
Additional illustrations: Andy Martin and Ed Roberts
Expert consultant: Juliet Mander
Americanization: Carrie Armstrong

The publisher would like to thank the following individuals and
organizations for photographs:
Cover – © Jerry Irwin/Science Photo Library;
p.1, 2/3, 10/11 – © Kit Houghton Photography/Corbis;
p.4/5 – © W. Perry Conway/Corbis; p.6/7 – © Peter Johnson/Corbis;
p.7(mr) – Digital Vision; p.12/13 – © Annie Griffiths Belt/Corbis;
p.14/15, p.18, p.19 – © Kit Houghton Photography;
p.16/17 – © Buddy Mays/Corbis.

First published in 2001 by Usborne Publishing Ltd.,
Usborne House, 83-85 Saffron Hill, London, EC1N 8RT, England.
www.usborne.com

First published in America 2004
Printed in Spain

CONTENTS

HOW TO USE THIS BOOK

This book is a guide to identifying horse and pony breeds from all over the world. The breeds are arranged with ponies first, followed by riding horses, harness horses (bred to pull light carriages) and draft horses (used for pulling heavy loads).

Next to each picture is a short description of the breed, telling you where it originated, what kind of work it was bred for, the colors it can be, and its height.

Some colors and markings have unusual names. You can look them up on page 9. If there are any other words you don't understand, look in the list of useful words on page 61, or check the diagram detailing horse parts on pages 10-11.

These horses live wild on the Great Plains in Wyoming, USA. They are descended from riding horses.

SPOTTING A BREED

When you see a breed, make a mark in the circle next to its description. Some types of horses only live in certain parts of the world, and others are very rare indeed. However, you might spot them in wildlife parks, in movies or on the television.

The chart on pages 62-63 lists every breed shown in this book. Note the date that you see each breed on the chart. You'll build up a record of the breeds that you've spotted.

Name of breed	Date
Dartmoor	8/6
Døle	8/6
Don	5/7
Dutch Draft	10/11

Fill in the chart like this.

THE STORY OF HORSES

The first horses were small and deer-like. They lived in woodlands, 50 million years ago. They evolved into swift, sure-footed beasts that were good at escaping from enemies.

All modern breeds of horse are descended from two ancient types, the southern type and the northern type.

Humans are thought to have begun to control and breed horses in Europe, several thousand years ago. Today, there are about 200 different breeds of horses.

The only truly wild breed left in the world is the Przewalski, from the Gobi Desert in Mongolia, where some still live in herds.

These horses' long legs and slender bodies are signs that they are descended from southern-type horses.

The southern type was light and swift, with a silky coat, like a modern Arab horse.

The northern type had a thick, rough coat and sturdy legs, like a modern Exmoor pony.

USING HORSES

Originally, horses were hunted for food. Later, they were bred for specific types of work. For example, some were bred to pull light carts and carriages day after day. Heavier types, meanwhile, were bred for plowing and pulling heavy carts and wagons.

Today, people ride mostly for pleasure or sport, although some horses still work on farms, especially in poorer countries.

In the 1800s Arab horses, which are small, nimble and swift, were crossed with English hunters, which are strong and hardy, to produce Thoroughbreds. This fast, tall and beautiful breed is now used for racing all over the world.

Racing Thoroughbreds

7

LOOKING AT HORSES

At first, it can be tricky to tell what breed a horse
or pony is. Here is a quick guide to certain clues.

A curved-in face (called a dished
profile) and a tail held high means
that the animal probably has some
Arab blood.

A small, sturdy build and a long,
rough coat are signs that it is
probably a mountain or
moorland pony.

A very tall, lightly built horse, with
long legs, a fine skin and coat is
probably a Thoroughbred.

A big, slow horse with heavy
features and feather (long hairs)
around its feet is probably a
draft horse.

CROSS OR PUREBRED?

Most horses and ponies are crossbred, that is,
descended from different types. You are likely to see
purebred horses and ponies at:

- Horse shows.
- Stud farms, where horses are bred.
- The breed's natural surroundings; for example, hills
  and moors in Britain, lowlands in France or Belgium,
  or mountains in Austria.
- Racing stable or racetracks.
- Riding stable.

COLORS AND MARKINGS

Here are nine of the most common coat colors and patterns, and the proper names for them.

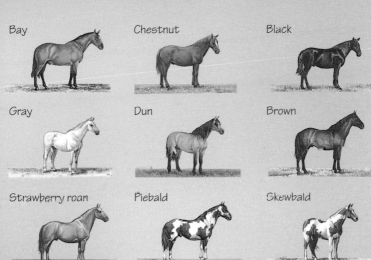

Bay

Chestnut

Black

Gray

Dun

Brown

Strawberry roan

Piebald

Skewbald

FACE MARKINGS

Star

Snip

Stripe

Blaze

LEG MARKINGS

Sock

Stocking

POINTS OF THE HORSE

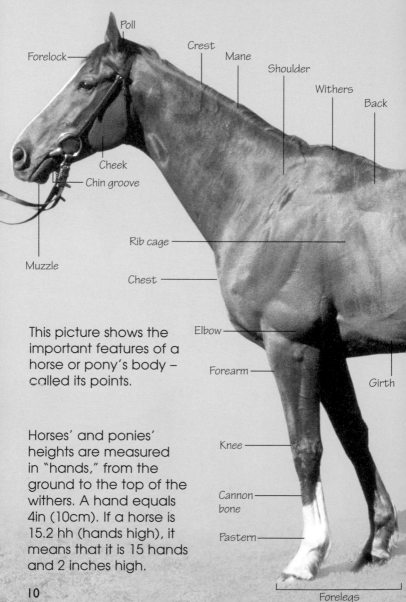

Poll

Crest

Mane

Shoulder

Withers

Back

Forelock

Cheek

Chin groove

Muzzle

Rib cage

Chest

Elbow

Forearm

Girth

Knee

Cannon bone

Pastern

Forelegs

This picture shows the important features of a horse or pony's body – called its points.

Horses' and ponies' heights are measured in "hands," from the ground to the top of the withers. A hand equals 4in (10cm). If a horse is 15.2 hh (hands high), it means that it is 15 hands and 2 inches high.

HORSE OR PONY?

Whether an animal is called a horse or a pony depends on how tall it is. If it is over 14.2 hands high (hh) then it is classed as a horse. If it is 14.2hh, or less, then it is called a pony.

Hindquarters

Loins

Hip

Croup

Dock

Tail

Flank

Thigh

Sheath

Hamstring

Stifle

Gaskin

Belly

Hock

Flowing hairs around the lower legs are called feather. This horse has slight feathering.

Coronet

Fetlock

Hoof

Hindlegs

HORSE AND PONY CARE

Wild horses and ponies live in groups, moving around together. To keep your horse or pony happy, let it live outside, as it would in the wild, as much as you can. To keep it healthy, follow these guidelines.

Ponies enjoy the freedom of outdoor life.

- Let it live in a field with other horses and ponies.
- Allow enough room for grazing. A pony needs at least 4000m^2 (one acre) to provide it with fresh grass.
- Change fields in spring and fall if the grass is thinning, to allow the grass to grow back.
- Clean up droppings.
- Provide plenty of fresh drinking water.
- Make sure that there is shelter in the field, such as trees, or a shed.
- Ensure that the field's fencing is strong, to stop escape attempts. Also, make sure that fencing is safe, to prevent injuries.

STABLING

During really cold winter spells, you should keep your animal in a barn. Follow these tips so that it stays happy and healthy.

• Exercise the animal every day. Ride for an hour, or turn it out into the field for a few hours.
• Feed it properly. It needs hay to nibble during the day and night, and high energy food such as corn, in the morning, at night and perhaps at noon.
• Give plenty of fresh water.
• Clean the stall daily. Remove wet bedding and droppings to stop smells and foot disease.

• Put down fresh bedding regularly.
• Groom the horse every day, to keep its coat and skin clean and healthy.
• If your animal is clipped, it will need to wear blankets in winter. Seek advice from an expert, so that you know just how much protection is needed.
• Always let fresh air into the barn to lessen the chances of your animal catching coughs and colds.
• If you want to change your feeding and exercising routines, alter them gradually. Horses and ponies don't like change. They need time to adjust to new ways.

13

FEEDING

In its natural environment, a horse or pony eats small amounts of bulk food (mostly grass) almost non-stop throughout the day. Those kept in stables eat hay instead of grass. During the summer, horses and ponies are kept outside, and probably need no food other than grass. However, during the winter, they need a supplement of hay.

EXTRA FEEDS

As well as hay or grass, a horse may need high energy or "short" feeds. Use corn or cubes, mixed with another type of food. (Corn is either oats or barley. Cubes are also called nuts.) You should seek advice from an expert about what would suit your animal best, and on how to prepare the food. Different horses have different needs.

Foods you can add to corn or cubes are:
• Bran, but only in small amounts.
• Chaff. This is made of chopped hay.
• Sugar beet, soaked for 24 hours prior to feeding.
• Small amounts of linseed, for a shiny coat.

FEEDING GUIDELINES

How much, and what, you give to your horse or pony will depend on its size, temperament, health, how much exercise it gets, the time of year, and how much good grass is available.

These are the basic rules for feeding:
• Always make sure that it has enough grass or hay to eat.
• Feed a little and often. It will not be able to digest large meals properly.

Horses should have access to fresh water, particularly at feeding time.

• Always have fresh drinking water available.
• Wait for at least an hour after feeding before you ride your horse or pony.
• Give feeds at the same time each day.
• If there's no grass, give juicy vegetables or fruits, such as carrots or apples.
• Make sure that you give the animal access to a salt block.

GROOMING

There are lots of grooming tools. Each has a different use. Here's a selection.

- A hoof pick is used for cleaning inside the hooves.

- Dirt and stains are taken off an unclipped coat with a dandy brush, working back from the top of the neck. Always brush in the direction of the coat.

- If the animal is kept in a barn, a body brush can be used to clean the skin and coat. Don't use this brush on a field-kept horse, though – it strips the body oils that keep the animal warm, dry and healthy.

- A sweat scraper removes excess sweat or water from the coat.

- A thin coat of hoof oil is brushed on the hooves to make them shine and stop them from splitting.

- Strapping pads are made of stuffed leather. Use them to groom the neck, shoulders and hind quarters, shortly after exercise. The pad shines the coat, and massages the muscles to tone them.

- A water brush is long and narrow, with short bristles. Used damp with water, for smoothing the mane and tail after brushing.

- Brushes are cleaned by pulling them across a rubber or metal currycomb.

SHOEING

Most working horses and ponies need to wear metal shoes to stop their hooves from getting worn down. Shoes also keep the hoof from becoming cracked, bruised or out of shape. Horseshoes must be made to fit properly, by a blacksmith – also called a farrier.

Unless a horse is being rested, new shoes should be fitted every 4-6 weeks. The shoes are nailed to the animal's hooves. It does not hurt, but some animals find the experience a little worrying at first.

PARTS OF THE HOOF

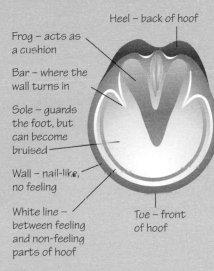

Heel – back of hoof

Frog – acts as a cushion

Bar – where the wall turns in

Sole – guards the foot, but can become bruised

Wall – nail-like, no feeling

White line – between feeling and non-feeling parts of hoof

Toe – front of hoof

PARTS OF A SHOE

Fullering

Nail hole

Pencil heels

Grooving

Toe clip

Shoes are shaped to fit the horse's feet before they are nailed into place.

RIDING

There are two main styles of riding:
• English style. This developed from an old European style of riding and is now practiced all over the world.
• Western style. This grew out of cattle ranching work in North and South America. Mostly it is used in the Americas for rodeo displays, modern ranch work and long-distance trail riding.

Riders of either style learn to sit so that the horse is well balanced and can move freely. They learn to control a horse using a combination of their hands, legs, body and voice.

If you would like to learn to ride, find a riding school that is approved by a horse society (details on page 60), so you can be sure that your teacher is qualified.

English-style riding

TACK

ENGLISH SADDLE
Also called a "General Purpose Saddle."

Cantle
Seat
Pommel
Stirrup iron
Saddle flap
Stirrup leather

SNAFFLE BRIDLE
One of several bridles used in English-style riding.

Browband
Headpiece
Throatlatch
Noseband
Cheekstrap
Bit
Rein

WESTERN SADDLE

WESTERN BRIDLE

Cheyenne roll
Cantle
Seat
Horn
Fork
Front jockey
Side jockey
Saddle strings
Fender
Wide tread stirrup

Browband
Throatlatch
Cheekpiece
Curb strap
Western curb bit
Rein

PONIES

⬇ HIGHLAND
Largest British pony. From the Scottish Highlands. Once used as a pack pony, now popular for trekking and driving. Usually gray or dun, can be black or chestnut. Up to 14.2hh.

Long, thick mane

Long, thick tail

Coat is long in winter

Thick, short neck

➡ SHETLAND
Smallest British pony. Used for riding and driving. Often black, brown or chestnut. Can be piebald or skewbald. About 9.2hh.

⬇ DALE
From the Pennine hills, northern England.
Used for pony trekking and as a harness
pony. Usually dark brown or
black. May have white
markings. Up to 14.2hh.

Lots of
feather

⬇ FELL
From higher regions of the western
Pennines. Usually black, sometimes
brown or bay. No white
markings. About 14hh.

PONIES

⬇ EXMOOR
Oldest British breed. Lives half wild on Exmoor, Southwest England. Hardy. Good riding pony. Bay or brown with light colored underside. Up to 12.3hh.

Rough, springy coat

Light colored muzzle

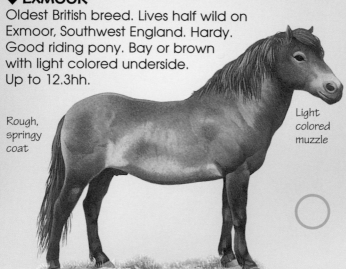

⬇ DARTMOOR
Lives half wild on Dartmoor, Southwest England. Hardy and sure-footed. Excellent riding pony. Bay, black or brown. About 12hh.

Small, pretty head

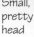

⬇ CONNEMARA

From Northwest Ireland. Ancestors probably Spanish and Arab horses. Jumps well. Usually gray, but often dun, black, brown, bay or chestnut. 13-14hh.

Elegant neck

⬅ NEW FOREST

From New Forest, southern England. Good riding pony. Size and markings vary, but not piebald or skewbald. Up to 14.2hh.

PONIES

⬇ WELSH MOUNTAIN

Old breed from Wales which has Arab and Thoroughbred blood. Popular show pony. Great for children. Usually gray or chestnut. Up to 12hh.

Tail carried high

Arab-type head

⬇ WELSH COB

Descended from Welsh ponies and Andalusian horses. Strong. Most colors, except piebald or skewbald. 14-15hh.

Arched neck

Deep, strong body

⬇ HAFLINGER

From the Tyrol mountains, Austria. Strong and sure footed. Ideal for pulling heavy loads on steep hillsides. Good for riding and driving in harness. Chestnut. About 14hh.

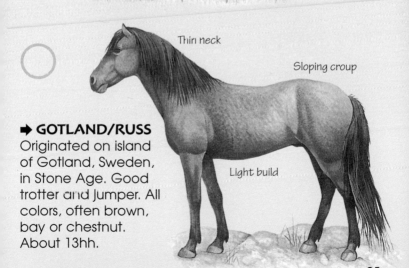

Heavy head

Flaxen (yellow) tail and mane

Thin neck

Sloping croup

➡ GOTLAND/RUSS

Originated on island of Gotland, Sweden, in Stone Age. Good trotter and jumper. All colors, often brown, bay or chestnut. About 13hh.

Light build

PONIES

⬇ ICELANDIC
Bred from various northern European ponies.
Used as riding or pack pony. Quiet and
friendly. Any color; often gray, dun,
brown, black or chestnut.
12-13hh.

Lifts knees
high when
moving

Black and silver mane and
tail. Mane grows short and
straight, like a crest.

➡ FJORD
Comes from
Norway. Good for
driving, haulage,
carrying and riding.
Mostly yellow-dun.
13-14hh.

➡ KAZAKH
From Russia. Used as
a long-distance racing
pony. Any color;
often bay, brown or
chestnut. About 13hh.

⬇ HUÇUL
From the Carpathian mountains of
Russia and Romania. Strong pack pony,
probably related to Tarpan breed.
Brown, dun or bay. About 13hh.

Short
neck

PONIES

⬇ CASPIAN
Wild pony, from Iran. Very few remaining.
Looks like a miniature Thoroughbred. Good
jumper. Usually bay or brown, sometimes
gray. Never has white marking.
9.2-11.2hh.

Long legs

Muscular
hindquarters

➡ CRIOLLO
From South America.
Survives well in
poor conditions.
Dun, roan, brown,
skewbald, black,
or bay. About 14.2hh.

⬇ CAMARGUE

From swampland at mouth of river Rhone, France. Tough and strong, many still live wild. Foals are born brown, but usually become gray. 14.2hh.

Large head

Coarse coat

Long, silky coat

➡ FALABELLA

Miniature horse, from Argentina. Not strong, but used as a driving pony and children's pet. Any color. Less than 7hh.

PONIES

⬇ PRZEWALSKI

Also called Asiatic or Mongolian Wild Horse. Only about 300 exist – either in captivity or in herds on Gobi Desert, Mongolia. Bay or dun. 12-14hh.

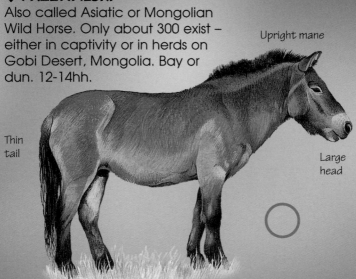

Upright mane

Thin tail

Large head

⬇ TARPAN

Oldest breed in Europe and northern Asia. Can be seen living wild in Poland. Usually brown with black ears, mane, tail and legs. 13hh.

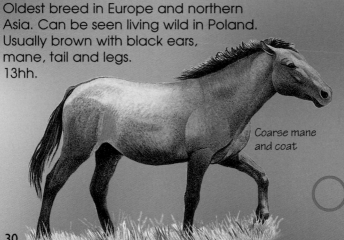

Coarse mane and coat

⬇ PONY OF THE AMERICAS

New breed, from the USA. Good riding pony. Spotted. Looks similar to Appaloosa horse, though smaller. 11.2-13.2hh.

Dark muzzle

Rounded body

⬇ SABLE ISLAND PONY

From Nova Scotia, Canada. Small and tough. Lives in wild herds. Feeds off scrub grass on sand dunes. Often chestnut. About 14hh.

Light build

31

RIDING HORSES

⬇ THOROUGHBRED
Bred in England from Arab
horses. World's fastest breed.
Powerful and elegant. Black,
brown, bay, gray or chestnut.
15-16.2hh.

High
withers

Neat
head

Long legs

Dished
profile

Tail carried high

➡ ANGLO-ARAB
Cross between
Thoroughbred
and Arab. Fast,
strong, handsome.
Excellent all-rounder.
Same markings as
Thoroughbred.
About 16hh.

⬇ APPALOOSA
Bred by native North Americans. Good in all uses. Markings vary, though mainly identified by spots and splashes of pink and white. 14-15.3hh.

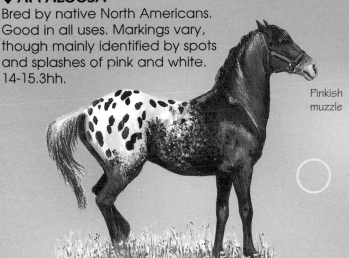

Pinkish muzzle

➡ AMERICAN SADDLEBRED
First bred as riding and harness horse in southern USA. An excellent riding horse. Bay, brown or chestnut. 15-15.3hh.

High tail

High knee action

RIDING HORSES

⬇ MORGAN

Originally bred from one American stallion named Justin Morgan. Solid, well-muscled. Bay, brown, black or chestnut.
14-15.2hh.

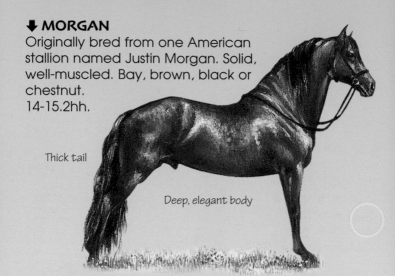

Thick tail

Deep, elegant body

⬇ TENNESSEE WALKING HORSE

From USA. Has three unusual gaits: flat-footed walk; running walk; running canter. Trots only when in harness. Solid markings.
15-16hh.

Head nods with each step

Long pasterns

➡ QUARTER HORSE
From USA. Named after quarter-mile races. Quick and intelligent. Any color. 15-16hh.

Short neck

Sloping croup

➡ PASO FINO
American, descended from Spanish explorers' horses. Does not trot at all. Can be any color. 13-15.2hh.

RIDING HORSES

⬇ SHAGYA ARAB
Eastern European horse bred from Arabs.
Tireless. Popular as cavalry horse in
World War One. Usually gray.
14-15hh.

Tail carried
high

Small, fine
head with
dished profile

Large eyes

Stong back

➡ POLISH ARAB
Bred in Poland since
1500. Used as general
riding horse and
racehorse. Tough and
strong. Popular in USA
and England. Can be
bay, gray or chestnut.
14.2-15.1hh.

Straight profile

Thick, arched neck

➡ ANDALUSIAN

From Southern Spain. Ancestors were Barb and Arab, plus native ponies. Good riding horse. Gray, black, bay or brown. 15.2-16hh.

⬇ LUSITANO

Portuguese horse. Same ancestry as Andalusian. Used by army, on farms and in bullrings. Gray, brown or bay. 15-16hh.

This horse is wearing special tack for the bullring.

RIDING HORSES

⬇ BUDYONNY

From Rostov, in Russia. Can live on poor food. Once used as a cavalry horse. Now often used for long-distance riding and racing. Brown, black, bay or chestnut. About 16hh.

Long neck

Upright shoulders

Strong legs

⬅ DON

Comes from the Don Valley, Russia. Survives well on poor grass. Has lots of stamina. Always chestnut. 15-16hh.

High, narrow body

Fine coat with metallic sheen

➡ AKHAL-TEKE
Ancient breed from Turkmenistan. Has many uses. Can stand great heat or cold. Golden chestnut, bay, black or gray. About 15.1hh.

⬇ KARABAIR
Comes from the mountains of central Asia. Fast and good natured. Can work in dry, hot weather. Equally good for riding or in harness. Gray, bay, black or chestnut. 14.2-15.2hh.

Fine, thin tail

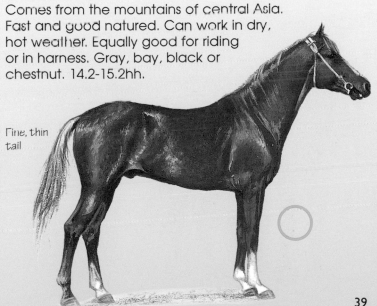

RIDING HORSES

⬇ PALOMINO

Popular in the USA. Descended from Arab horses. The name can refer either to the breed or the color. Mostly bred as show horses. Any shade of chestnut, with white mane and tail. 14-16hh.

Often has white face markings

Overo marking type

⬅ PINTO

Bred in the USA. There are two marking types: overo and tobiano. Overo is mostly dark, with white patches. Tobiano is mostly white, and has dark patches. Various heights.

➡ TURKOMAN

Comes from
Turkmenistan and
northern Iran.
Strong and tireless.
Good riding horse.
Usually gray or bay;
but also dun or
chestnut. 14.3-15.2hh.

Long neck

Straight
nose

⬇ TRAKEHNER

Bred mainly in Poland and Germany.
Used as a farm and cavalry horse.
Gentle but brave. Very good
sports horse. Bay, brown, black
or chestnut. 16-16.2hh.

Sloping
shoulders

41

RIDING HORSES

↓ DØLE/GUDBRANDSAAL
Also called Ostland or Dølehest.
From Norway. Strong, medium size.
Originally used as a pack horse.
Usually black, brown or bay.
About 15hh.

Strong
neck

Lots of
feather

➡ SELLE FRANCAIS
Crossbred in France
from Anglo-Arab and
other horses. Brave
and strong. Excellent
for riding and sports,
especially jumping.
Often chestnut.
15.2-16.3hh.

⬇ HANOVERIAN

German breed descended from war horses ridden in the Middle Ages. Strong. Good sports horse. Any solid color; often bay or brown. 16-17hh.

Strong hindquarters

Heavy shoulders

➡ HOLSTEIN

German breed. Big and strong. A good carriage and sports horse. Usually brown, bay or black. 16-16.2hh.

43

RIDING HORSES

➡ KNABSTRUP

Danish breed
descended from
a spotted Spanish
mare. Popular as
a circus horse.
Fast and hardy.
Always spotted,
usually white with
black spots.
About 15hh.

Short,
arched neck

⬅ LIPIZZANER

Used by the famous Spanish
Riding School, Vienna, Austria.
Bred from Andalusian horses.
Excellent dressage horse;
also good in harness.
Born brown or
black, changes
to gray. Pure
white in old age.
15-15.2hh.

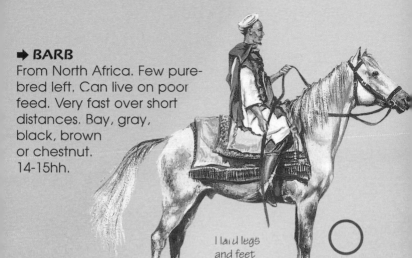

➡ BARB

From North Africa. Few pure-bred left, Can live on poor feed. Very fast over short distances. Bay, gray, black, brown or chestnut. 14-15hh.

Hard legs and feet

High withers

Narrow hindquarters

➡ WALER

First bred in New South Wales, Australia. Originally a cavalry horse. Now used for cattle herding, rodeos, show jumping and general riding. Any solid color. 15-16hh.

HARNESS HORSES

➡ STANDARDBRED
Trotting horse, from the USA. The name comes from the fact that trotting horses had to achieve a certain speed, the "standard," before they were allowed to race. Any solid color; usually bay, black or brown. 15-16hh.

Long body

Long back

➡ ORLOV TROTTER
From Russia, named after Count Orlov. Strong and fairly heavy. Once used as a cavalry horse. Often gray, also black or bay. 15.2-17hh.

Some feather

46

Thick, curly
mane and tail

➡ FRIESIAN

From Friesland, in
the Netherlands.
Bred in the Middle
Ages to carry
knights in armor.
Strong and good
natured. Always
black. About
15hh.

⬇ GELDERLANDER

From Gelderland, in Netherlands.
Once worked on farms. Now used for
riding and harness work. Chestnut,
gray, bay or brown. 15.2-16hh.

Tail
carried
high

Wide body

HARNESS HORSES

➡ GRONINGEN
Farm horse, from the Netherlands. Heavy, but fast. Can live on poor food. Good in harness or for riding. Usually black, bay or brown. 15.2-16hh.

Deep, strong body

➡ OLDENBURGER
From Northwest Germany. Big, strong, fairly fast. Popular carriage horse, used for riding, too. Usually gray, bay, black or brown. 16.2-17.2hh.

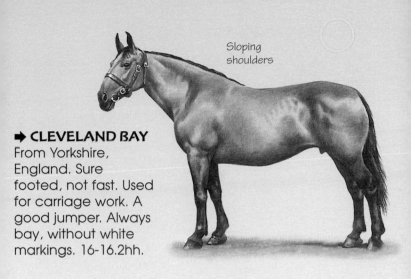

Sloping shoulders

➡ CLEVELAND BAY
From Yorkshire, England. Sure footed, not fast. Used for carriage work. A good jumper. Always bay, without white markings. 16-16.2hh.

⬇ HACKNEY
English, high stepping trotter, famous for exaggerated but graceful action. Popular at horse shows, it is often used to pull light carriages. Bay, black or brown. 14.3-15.3hh.

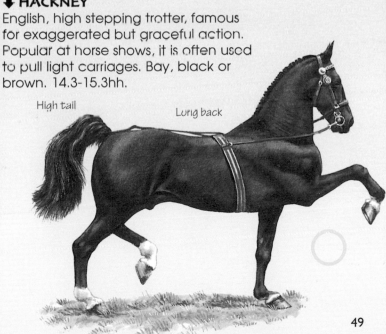

High tail

Long back

HARNESS HORSES

⬇ KUSTANAIR

From Kazakhstan, Central Asia. Three types: Steppe, Riding and Basic. The Steppe is heavy and slow, Riding is light, and the Basic is between the two. Has solid colors, usually chestnut or bay. 15-15.2hh.

This is the lighter, "Basic" type of Kustanair.

➡ FINNISH

Mainly used on farms and in forests in Finland. Gentle and tireless. Also used for trotting races and riding. Most are chestnut, often with white markings. About 15.2hh.

50

➡ FREDERIKSBORG

An old breed from
Denmark. Hard
working. Used on farms
and for riding. Srong and
lively. Usually chestnut.
Up to 16hh.

Short legs

⬇ KLADRUBER

From Czech and Slovak regions of Europe.
First bred in sixteenth century, for Emperor
Maximilian II. Often used on farms
and in dressage competitions.
Black or gray. 16-17hh.

Prominent,
curved
nose

HARNESS HORSES

⬇ NONIUS
Hungarian. Named after an Anglo-Norman stallion that founded the breed. Black, bay or brown. Has a large size range – from 14.2-17hh.

Small eyes

This is the "Light" type of Wielkopolski

➡ WIELKOPOLSKI
Polish. Many types: heavy ones are used on farms; light ones to drive or ride. Usually bay, brown or chestnut. About 16hh.

DRAFT HORSES

➡ CLYDESDALE
Scottish. Strong and active, but not very heavy. Popular on farms. Bay, brown or black, with white on feet, face and underside. About 17hh.

⬇ SHIRE
The classic English draft horse. Once carried knights in armor. Later used on farms and to pull heavy loads, such as beer wagons. Hard worker, usually bay, black or gray, with white markings. Up to 18hh.

Lots of feather

53

DRAFT HORSES

➡ SUFFOLK PUNCH
From Suffolk, England. Short and stocky. Does well on little or poor food. Very good natured. Always chestnut. About 16-16.2hh.

Thick neck

Wide chest

⬅ IRISH DRAFT
Good all-round farm horse, from Ireland. Makes a very good sports horse when crossed with a Thoroughbred. Bay, gray, chestnut or brown. 15.2-17hh.

Silky, dapple gray coat

➡ PERCHERON

From Northern France. A popular working horse. Very strong. Often weighs over a ton, but needs little food. Good to work with. Black or gray. 15.2-17hh.

Heavy neck and shoulders

⬅ ARDENNES

From France and Belgium. Was used by Napoleon's cavalry. Powerful but gentle. Can live out in bad weather. Chestnut, roan or bay. About 15.2-16hh.

DRAFT HORSES

⬇ BRETON HEAVY DRAFT

From northwest France. A strong, rugged working horse. Usually strawberry roan in color, but can be bay or chestnut. 15-16hh.

➡ PINZGAUER NORIKER

The oldest Austrian breed. Quiet and strong. Excellent for pulling plows. Bay, chestnut or spotted. 15-16hh.

Short legs

Arched neck

➡ AUXOIS

Ancient French breed. Once used for carriage and farm work. A powerful working horse. Usually bay or strawberry roan. Never black or gray. About 15.2hh.

Muscular body

⬅ TRAIT DU NORD

From northern France. Similar in shape and temperament to the Ardennes. Quiet and gentle. Usually bay, roan or chestnut. About 16hh.

DRAFT HORSES

➡ AVELIGNESE
Bred mainly in Tuscany, northern Italy. Originally used as a pack pony or a light draft horse. Short and muscular. Usually chestnut. About 14.2hh.

Flaxen (yellow) mane and tail

⬅ VLADIMIR
From Vladimir, Russia. Used for heavy and light harness work. Bay, roan or chestnut. About 16hh.

Very deep body

➡ JUTLAND
Danish. Once used by the Vikings. Mostly used as a farm horse and as a brewers' draft horse. Chestnut, black, gray, bay or light brown. 15.2-15.3hh.

Very short legs

➡ SCHLESWIG

From Northern Germany. Once used to carry knights in armor. Now used mostly on farms, and for haulage. Almost always chestnut. 15.2-16hh.

⬅ DUTCH DRAFT

An ancient, purebreed. Traditionally used on Dutch farms. Very placid. Strong and hard working. Gray, bay or chestnut. Up to 16.3hh.

Short head

Dapple gray color

➡ BOULONNAIS

Bred in France for the Crusades. Later used as a farm horse. Strong and good looking. Gray, bay or black. About 16.2hh.

WEBSITES

If you have access to the Internet, you can visit these websites to find out more about horses and ponies. For links to these sites, go to the Usborne Quicklinks Website at **www.usborne-quicklinks.com** and enter the keywords "spotters horses".

Internet safety
When using the Internet, please follow the **Internet safety guidelines** shown on the Usborne Quicklinks Website.

GENERAL WEBSITES

WEBSITE 1 Lots of detailed information for horse enthusiasts.

WEBSITE 2 Online exhibits of the history of the horse.

WEBSITE 3 A guide to horse and pony breeds.

WEBSITE 4 The fossil history of horses.

WEBSITE 5 Useful information on a wide variety of subjects, from feeding to schooling.

PONY CLUBS

The Pony Club is an ideal starting place for young people interested in riding. It has over 100,000 members worldwide.

WEBSITES 1-4 Links to Pony Clubs in the UK, Australia, Canada and the USA.

GOVERNING BODIES

WEBSITE 1 The Fédération Equestre Internationale, the world's governing body for equestrianism.

WEBSITES 2-7 Links to the Equestrian Federations of the UK, Ireland, USA, Canada, Australia and New Zealand.

USEFUL WORDS

all rounder – horse or pony that is good at different things, such as hunting and gymkhana games.

cob – short, stocky horse (about 15.3hh). Quiet and well behaved.

colt – male horse up to three years old.

dressage – training of a horse to master basic skills plus more difficult, precision movements

event horse – used in horse trials, which include dressage, show jumping and cross-country riding.

filly – female horse up to three years old.

flat racing – racing over short course without jumps.

foal – horse or pony up to one year old.

gelding – male horse that has been operated on so that it cannot breed.

gymkhana – show where short races and mounted games are held.

horse – fully grown horse that is over 14.2hh.

hunter – strong horse that can gallop cross-country and jump fences.

hurdler – horse that races and jumps small barriers, called hurdles, usually over courses about 4km (2½ miles) long.

mare – female horse over three years old.

pony – fully grown horse that is under 14.2hh.

school master – old, well-behaved, well-schooled horse or pony. Safe and reliable for people learning to ride.

show jumping – jumping competitions.

show horse/pony – competes at horse shows in one, or several, classes of competition. Judged on its appearance and schooling as well as suitability for the class entered.

stallion – male horse (not a gelding) more than three years old. Can be very difficult to control.

steeplechase – race run over fences on courses about 4 miles (7km) long. Name comes from old English tradition of racing between church steeples.

SPOTTER'S CHART

The horses and ponies on this chart are arranged in alphabetical order. When you see one, write down the date in the blank space next to each name. You might like to jot down the name of the place where you saw it, too, for a more complete record of your spotting.

Name of breed	Date	Name of breed	Date
Akhal-Teke		Connemara	
American Saddlebred		Criollo	
Andalusian		Dale	
Anglo-Arab		Dartmoor	
Appaloosa		Døle	
Arab (any type)		Don	
Ardennes		Dutch Draft	
Auxois		Exmoor	
Avelignese		Falabella	
Barb		Fell	
Boulonnais		Finnish	
Breton		Fjord	
Budyonny		Fredericksborg	
Camargue		Friesian	
Caspian		Gelderlander	
Cleveland Bay		Gotland	
Clydesdale		Groningen	

Name of breed	Date	Name of breed	Date
Hackney		Pinto	
Haflinger		Pinzgauer Noriker	
Hanoverian		Pony of the Americas	
Highland		Przewalski	
Holstein		Quarter Horse	
Huçul		Sable Island	
Icelandic		Schleswig	
Irish Draft		Shetland	
Jutland		Shire	
Karabair		Standardbred	
Kazakh		Suffolk Punch	
Kladruber		Tarpan	
Knabstrup		Tennessee Walking Horse	
Kustanair		Thoroughbred	
Lipizzaner		Trait du Nord .	
Lusitano		Trakehner	
Morgan		Turkoman	
New Forest		Vladimir	
Nonius		Waler	
Oldenburger		Welsh Cob	
Orlov Trotter		Welsh Mountain	
Palomino		Wielkopolski	
Paso Fino			
Percheron			

INDEX